THE BENEFITS OF PRAYING IN
TONGUES DURING TIMES OF CRISIS

YOUR END TIMES
PRAYER
SECRET

JENNIFER
LECLAIRE

©Copyright, 2020 — Jennifer LeClaire

Unless otherwise identified, Scripture quotations are taken from the New King James Version. Copyright © 1982 by Thomas Nelson, Inc. Used by permission. All rights reserved. Scripture quotations marked AMPC are taken from the Amplified® Bible, Classic Edition, Copyright © 1954, 1958, 1962, 1964, 1965, 1987 by The Lockman Foundation. All rights reserved. Used by permission. Scripture quotations marked ESV are taken from The Holy Bible, English Standard Version® (ESV®), copyright © 2001 by Crossway, a publishing ministry of Good News Publishers. Used by permission. All rights reserved. Scripture quotations marked KJV are taken from the King James Version. Scripture quotations marked NASB are taken from the NEW AMERICAN STANDARD BIBLE®, Copyright © 1960,1962,1963,1968, 1971,1972,1973,1975,1977,1995 by The Lockman Foundation. Used by permission. Scripture quotations marked TPT are taken from *The Passion Translation*, Copyright © 2014, 2015, 2016, 2017, www.thepassiontranslation.com. Used by permission of BroadStreet Publishing Group, LLC, Racine, Wisconsin, USA. All rights reserved. Scripture quotations marked NLT are taken from the Holy Bible, New Living Translation, copyright 1996, 2004, 2015. Used by permission of Tyndale House Publishers., Wheaton, Illinois 60189. All rights reserved. Scripture quotations marked MSG are taken from *The Message*. Copyright © 1993, 1994, 1995, 1996, 2000, 2001, 2002. Used by permission of NavPress Publishing Group. Scripture quotations marked CEV are taken from the Contemporary English Version Copyright © 1995 by the

American Bible Society, New York, NY. All rights reserved. Scripture quotations marked GNT are taken from the Good News Translation, Second Edition, Copyright 1992 by American Bible Society. Used by Permission. Scripture quotations marked MEV are taken from *The Holy Bible, Modern English Version*. Copyright © 2014 by Military Bible Association. Published and distributed by Charisma House. All rights reserved. Used by permission. Scripture quotations marked NHEB are taken from the New Heart English Bible, edited by Wayne A. Mitchell, 2008. Public Domain.

All emphasis within Scripture quotations is the author's own.

DESTINY IMAGE® PUBLISHERS, INC.
PO Box 310, Shippensburg, PA 17257-0310
"Promoting Inspired Lives"

This book and all other Destiny Image and Destiny Image Fiction books are available at Christian bookstores and distributors worldwide.

For more information on foreign distributors, call 717-532-3040.

Or reach us on the Internet: www.destinyimage.com

ISBN 13 TP: 978-0-7684-5691-2

ISBN 13 eBook: 978-0-7684-5692-9

For Worldwide Distribution, Printed in the U.S.A.

1 2 3 4 5 6 / 23 22 21 20

Contents

Chapter 1: Signs of the Time Are All Around Us 7

Chapter 2: The Whole Creation Is Groaning . . 21

Chapter 3: Supernatural Prayer that Births Endurance 31

Chapter 4: Getting Filled with the Spirit 63

Chapter 5: Prophecies to War With 75

About the Author 85

Chapter 1
Signs of the Times Are All Around Us

While some Christian prognosticators make too much out of too little—and even secular media like *The New York Times* are publishing tantalizing articles with headlines like "The Apocalypse as an 'Unveiling': What Religion Teaches Us About the End Times"—we shouldn't be too quick to dismiss what the Bible says about the grand finale of the earth as we know it.

Put another way, it's clear the end of the age is not at hand—but it doesn't take a prophet to see the signs of the times manifesting before our very eyes. Events from the pages of the Bible we carry to church and read on our digital devices are truly unfolding and the discerning are taking note of the trends to which Scripture pointed.

This is the right response. In fact, Jesus expected us to discern the age. Did you know He actually rebuked the Pharisees for not discerning the signs of the times at His first coming over 2,000 years ago? He wants His people to be in tune with Him and expects us to see the signs of His Second Coming. That means knowing the Word. Matthew 16:1-4 reads:

Then the Pharisees and Sadducees came, and testing Him asked that He would show them a sign from heaven. He answered and said to them, 'When it is evening you say, "It will be fair weather, for the sky is red"; and in the morning, "It will be foul weather today, for the sky is red and threatening." Hypocrites! You know how to discern the face of the sky, but you cannot discern the signs of the times. A wicked and adulterous generation seeks after a sign, and no sign shall be given to it except the sign of the prophet Jonah.' And He left them and departed.

Understanding the signs of the times is not an endeavor for a few eschatologists or televangelists. Discerning times is critical to our walk with God. If we don't discern the times, we won't respond rightly. We won't pray rightly. And we might get offended at God and fall away.

We need to be spiritually prepared and educated in the whole counsel of God, including the signs of the end times. We need to understand God's plan for the end of the age and come to know aspects of Christ we may have ignored. We need to be aware of the signs so we can pray in agreement with the Lord's will that His Kingdom come and His will be done on earth as it is in heaven (see Matt. 6:9-10). What's more, understanding the signs of the times guards us from deception, inspires us to live holy, and urges us to preach the gospel.

In Matthew 24:32-35, Jesus said, *"Now learn this parable from the fig tree: When its branch has already become tender and puts forth leaves, you know that summer is near. So you also, when you see all these things, know that it is near—at the doors! Assuredly, I say to you, this generation will by no means pass away till all these things take place. Heaven and earth will pass away, but My words will by no means pass away."*

And, again, Jesus was clear: *"Take heed to yourselves, lest your hearts be weighed down with carousing, drunkenness, and cares of this life, and that Day come on you unexpectedly. For it will come as a snare on all those who dwell on the face of the whole earth. Watch therefore, and pray always that you may be counted worthy to escape all these things that will come to pass, and to stand before the Son of Man"* (Luke 21:34-36).

Do You See the Signs?

Some believers may shy away from studying the signs of the times because of poor predictions about the timing of Christ's return and overblown publicity over a blood moon. Remember Edgar C. Whisenant's *88*

Reasons Why the Rapture Will Be in 1988? Or the late Harold Camping's continual time-stamped predictions that never occurred?

These predictions were flawed, in part, because Jesus Himself said, *"But of that day and hour no one knows, not even the angels of heaven, but My Father only. But as the days of Noah were, so also will the coming of the Son of Man be"* (Matt. 24:36-37). Nevertheless, the signs of the times are all around us. In his book *Israel in Prophecy*, John Walvoord wrote:

> Never before in history have all factors been present for fulfillment of prophecy relating to end-time trends and events. Only in our generation have combined revival of Israel, formation of world church, increasing power of Muslim religion, rise of occult, worldwide spread

of atheism as dramatic setting for fulfillment of prophecy. The road to Armageddon is prepared. The advent of globalism and technologies linking communications and cash systems, the growing spiritual apostasy worldwide, with longing for leader who can unite diverse religious and political factions are setting stage for Antichrist one-world government.[1]

You can see Scripture unfold before your eyes—and signs of the times that correlated to chapter and verse—through what many call "sign events." Sign events are events Scripture predicts that point to the timing of Christ's Second Coming. One of the greatest sign events in the history of the world is the rebirth of Israel, which happened in 1948.

Ezekiel 38:8, as well as many other Scriptures, point to this critical event in human history: *"After many days you will be visited. In the latter years you will come into the land of those brought back from the sword and gathered from many people on the mountains of Israel, which had long been desolate; they were brought out of the nations, and now all of them dwell safely."*

There are, however, sign events that have yet to take place, such as the abomination of desolation scribed in Revelation 13:14. This is when the Antichrist sets himself up as a god for people to worship. The Antichrist has not yet been revealed, nor has the covenant of peace been inked despite decades of peace talks in the Middle East. Israel's land has been the focus of a spiritual war for thousands of years. Only the Antichrist will successfully broker a peace treaty in the Middle East.

What Christ Said About the End Times

Sign trends are a little more obscure. They are not as black and white as sign events. Still, Scripture points to sign trends, and we're seeing the rise and rapidity of these trends Christ and others mentioned in the Gospels and Epistles. Jesus had plenty to say about the end times. In Matthew 24:4-14, He was clear:

> *Take heed that no one deceives you. For many will come in My name, saying, 'I am the Christ,' and will deceive many. And you will hear of wars and rumors of wars. See that you are not troubled; for all these things must come to pass, but the end is not yet. For nation will rise against nation, and kingdom*

against kingdom. And there will be famines, pestilences, and earthquakes in various places. All these are the beginning of sorrows. Then they will deliver you up to tribulation and kill you, and you will be hated by all nations for My name's sake. And then many will be offended, will betray one another, and will hate one another. Then many false prophets will rise up and deceive many. And because lawlessness will abound, the love of many will grow cold. But he who endures to the end shall be saved. And this gospel of the kingdom will be preached in all the world as a witness to all the nations, and then the end will come.

But He didn't stop there. In Luke 21:11, He said, "And there will be great earthquakes in various places, and famines and pestilences; and there will be fearful sights and great signs from heaven." And in Luke 21:25 He said, "And there will be signs in the sun, in the moon, and in the stars; and on the earth distress of nations, with perplexity, the sea and the waves roaring."

Secular news headlines point to the sign trends. Just Google terms like *ethnic conflict, economic warfare, famines,* and *persecution*. Ethnic conflict is real—nation is rising against nation. Economic warfare is raging—kingdom is rising against kingdom. There are real wars, real famines, real earthquakes, real deception, real persecution of believers, real lawlessness, real fearful sights, and real disturbances in the sea. And there are real pestilences.

Is Coronavirus a Sign of the Times?

A pestilence is a contagious or infections epidemic disease that is virulent and devastating, according to *Merriam-Webster's Dictionary*. Coronavirus, or COVID-19, would qualify. And this is one of the clear markers of the end times.

Of course, coronavirus is not the first health scare of the last two decades—and it will not be the last. We've seen H1N1, or the swine flu. Then there was H5N1, the bird flu. Remember Severe Acute Respiratory Syndrome, or SARS? Fewer remember Methicillin-Resistant Staphylococcus Aureus (MRSA), but the medical world called it major threat. Then there was Ebola and, going further back, HIV. During this century we've seen the Russian Flu, the Hong Kong Flu, the Spanish Flu. And plagues are nothing new to the 20th and 21st centuries. There were great plagues in the 19th century and even earlier.

Signs of the Times Are All Around Us

In fact, pestilences go back to the book of Exodus. *Pestilence* appears in the New King James Version of the Bible 44 times. All but two mentions of pestilence take place in the Old Testament. In other words, God isn't sending pestilence as judgment in the New Testament and we won't see Him use pestilence as a judgment until we enter the times of the Book of Revelation—but plagues are listed as a sign of the times. The Hebrew word for pestilence is a contagious or infectious epidemic disease that is virulent and devastating.

Coronavirus is a pestilence and it is a sign of the times. The world is in crisis. But this wasn't the first virus and it won't be the last. This is not the first sign of the times and it won't be the last. Pestilences will rise with more rapidity and are a marker of the end times before the Second Coming of the

Lord Jesus Christ. Remember, He said in Matthew 24:7: *"And there will be famines, pestilences, and earthquakes in various places."*

As we walk in the word and pray, God will deliver us from pestilence. Psalm 91:3 heralds: *"Surely He shall deliver you from the snare of the fowler and from the perilous pestilence."* And Psalm 91:5-6 tells us: *"You shall not be afraid of the terror by night, nor of the arrow that flies by day, nor of the pestilence that walks in darkness, nor of the destruction that lays waste at noonday."* Prayer can cause the pestilence to come to a halt before it crosses your threshold. Praying in tongues is part of your spiritual arsenal in times of crisis.

Note

1. John Walvoord, *Israel in Prophecy* (Grand Rapids, MI: Zondervan, 1962), 129.

Chapter 2
The Whole Creation
Is Groaning

Paul offered apocalyptic language in the eighth chapter of Romans. Before the apostle explained how the Holy Spirit helps our weaknesses because we don't know how to pray as we ought—and before he encouraged us with the revelation that the Holy Spirit Himself makes intercession for us with groanings that cannot be uttered—he talked about a different kind of groaning.

For the earnest expectation of the creation eagerly waits for the revealing of the sons of God. For the creation was subjected to futility, not willingly, but because of Him who subjected it in hope; because the creation itself also will be delivered from the bondage of corruption into the glorious liberty of the children of God. For we know that the whole creation groans and labors with birth pangs together until now. Not only that, but we also who have the firstfruits of the Spirit, even we ourselves groan within ourselves, eagerly waiting for the adoption, the redemption of our body (Romans 8:19-23).

When man fell in the Garden of Eden, the whole creation felt the effects of sin. Just like the rocks would cry out in praise if humans fail to praise Him (see Luke 19:40), the whole earth is travailing until

The Whole Creation Is Groaning

the Second Coming of Christ when the new heaven and new earth will manifest. Even if intercessors aren't travailing, the earth is. Indeed, when the Bible says the whole creation groans it speaks of extreme pain, agony, extreme and continued suffering, according to *Barnes' Notes on the Bible*. The world is waiting for deliverance.

What do the birth pains look like? Geopolitical, geophysical, astrophysical, socio-economic events—and plagues. The birth pains look like the signs of the times. Think about a woman in labor. She has her first contraction, but that doesn't mean much. Sometimes contractions—known as Braxton Hicks contractions—signal false labor. It's not until the contractions are consistent that a woman goes to the hospital to deliver. As the time of birthing comes closer, the birth pains—the contractions—grow nearer until the deliverance finally occurs and something new is born.

The whole creation is groaning for deliverance and the manifestations of the sons of God who will rule and reign with Christ in the new earth because creation will be restored to its first beauty. As the pain of waiting intensifies, the groaning becomes louder.

The Pain Is Intensifying

When Jesus' disciples came to Him privately and asked about the sign of His Second Coming and the end of the age, Jesus answered: *"See that no one leads you astray. For many will come in my name, saying, 'I am the Christ,' and they will lead many astray. And you will hear of wars and rumors of wars. See that you are not alarmed, for this must take place, but the end is not yet. For nation will rise against nation, and kingdom against kingdom, and there will be famines and earthquakes in various places. All these are but the beginning of the birth pains"* (Matt. 24:4-8 ESV).

With plagues hitting the earth that have killed millions and infected millions more, the pains are growing more severe. With lockdowns, shut ins, and social distancing, the pain of isolation is also real. With famines and the threat of nuclear war looming over our heads, fearful sights are all around us. The birth pains are coming more rapidly.

Paul also spoke to the church at Thessalonica about the pain: *"But concerning the times and the seasons, brethren, you have no need that I should write to you. For you yourselves know perfectly that the day of the Lord so comes as a thief in the night. For when they say, 'Peace and safety!' then sudden destruction comes upon them, as labor pains upon a pregnant woman. And they shall not escape"* (1 Thess. 5:1-3).

Earth Is Groaning Louder in Israel

When I led a team to the Holy Land in February, the Holy Spirit spoke these words to me: "The earth is groaning louder in Israel." I shared it with a few people and have been praying on it. I knew immediately the Holy Spirit was pointing me to Romans 8:19-23 (AMPC):

> *For [even the whole] creation* (all nature) *waits expectantly and longs earnestly for God's sons to be made known [waits for the revealing, the disclosing of their sonship]. For the creation* (nature) *was subjected to frailty* (to futility, condemned to

The Whole Creation Is Groaning

frustration), not because of some intentional fault on its part, but by the will of Him Who so subjected it—[yet] with the hope that nature (creation) *itself will be set free from its bondage to decay and corruption [and gain an entrance] into the glorious freedom of God's children. We know that the whole creation [of irrational creatures] has been moaning together in the pains of labor until now. And not only the creation, but we ourselves too, who have and enjoy the firstfruits of the [Holy] Spirit [a foretaste of the blissful things to come] groan inwardly as we wait for the redemption of our bodies [from sensuality and the grave, which will reveal] our adoption* (our manifestation as God's sons).

The whole creation includes the earth, stars, plants, animals, and human beings. But the Holy Spirit specifically pointed to the earth groaning in Israel, and even louder in Israel than in other places. What does this mean? It signals we're edging closer to the return of the Lord Jesus Christ. After Joel prophesied about God pouring out His spirit on all flesh and people prophesying and having dreams and visions in Joel 2:28-29, he prophesied about the end times in verses 30-32:

> *And I will show wonders in the heavens and in the earth: blood and fire and pillars of smoke. The sun shall be turned into darkness, and the moon into blood, before the coming of the great and awesome day of the Lord. And it shall come to pass that whoever calls on the name of the Lord shall be saved. For in Mount Zion and in Jerusalem there shall be deliverance, as the Lord*

has said, among the remnant whom the Lord calls.

Israel's Groan

So why is the earth groaning louder in Israel? Israel is center stage of the world. All eyes are on Israel. International media is stationed in Israel waiting and watching. This is where the Messiah will return. Here's what we know. God always hears Israel's groaning. Over and over again in Scripture, God hears her groans and responds. He always hears her cries for deliverance.

The Holy Spirit told me, "The earth is groaning louder in Israel." I am still praying through this, but what I know is the sons of God need to rise up. God is coming back for a glorious bride without spot or wrinkle (see Eph. 5:27). That means there's some sifting in store, some falling away to witness, some false prophets to avoid, and some evangelism to do.

After the birth pangs, something else happens. Jesus said, *"Then they will deliver you up to tribulation and kill you, and you will be hated by all nations for My name's sake. And then many will be offended, will betray one another, and will hate one another. Then many false prophets will rise up and deceive many. And because lawlessness will abound, the love of many will grow cold. But he who endures to the end shall be saved. And this gospel of the kingdom will be preached in all the world as a witness to all the nations, and then the end will come"* (Matt. 24:9-14).

I do not know when the Lord is returning, but I know we're a day closer than we were yesterday. And I know the earth in Israel is groaning loudly.

Chapter 3
Supernatural Prayer that Births Endurance

While on my morning prayer call, I felt the Holy Spirit stirring me. Suddenly, I released a pivotal prophecy for the Body of Christ. I didn't know it at the time, but He was preparing us for a time of world crisis, urging us to dig a deeper well within and to build ourselves up in our most holy faith by praying in the Spirit (see Jude 20). This is the prophecy that set off *Transform: The 90-Day Spirit Prayer Challenge* on schoolofthespirit.tv and got thousands of people around the world praying in tongues for one hour a day:

> Pray in My Spirit and I will do a work on the inside of you that will birth miracles in you and miracles through you. Pray in the Spirit. That is the master key that so many of My children are missing. For they read the Word, read the Word, read the Word, read the Word, which does so much good in their soul, but when they begin to pray in the Spirit in conjunction with reading the Word a revival begins to break out in their heart that spills over into their words, into their cities and churches, and the lost begin to take notice.
>
> I'm supercharging you even now as you pray in the Spirit. So do not delay by putting off this vital aspect

Supernatural Prayer that Births Endurance

of your life in Christ any longer. But begin to walk like He walked as you talk like He talked and think like He thinks and pray like He prayed, going off to secret places early in the morning, waiting on Me for direction, only doing what He saw Me do.

Do it My way. I won't do it your way, but I'll help you do it My way. I have a life of power, of prophetic wonder for you. So stand firm in My promises and do not budge form the place that I've called you to stand, and pray in the Spirit and speak the Word only and watch what happens when you combine this with that, the Word with the Spirit. Watch the revival that breaks out in your heart and in your mind, in your soul, in your emotions, every bit of you.

You will begin to burn and shine for Me and the world will stand up and take notice.

Over the next 90 days, if you will commit yourself to praying in the Sprit full on, I will do miracles on the inside of you and I will even change circumstances on the outside. If you'll just pray in the Spirit, you'll see that some of those circumstances on the outside won't bother you on the inside and some of those things on the inside will have to come out and go to the outside because they don't belong in you. And if you'll let Me mortify that inner life, the part that is warring against My Spirit, those places that are infiltrated by the enemy's lies, you will see new life spring forth. Ninety days to better you.

The testimonies from this 90-day prayer challenge at schoolofthespirit.tv even shocked me. People were delivered from demons. Bodies were healed. Debts were cancelled. Families restored. The Holy Spirit is a multi-tasker. He can do many things at the same times when we pray in tongues.

When You Don't Know How to Pray

Paul offers a revelation that can change your entire prayer life—and your entire life—in Romans 8:26-27: *"Likewise, the Spirit helps us in our weaknesses, for we do not know what to pray for as we ought, but the Spirit Himself intercedes for us with groanings too deep for words. He who searches the hearts knows what the mind of the Spirit is, because He intercedes for the saints according to the will of God"* (MEV).

We may think we know how to pray in a time of crisis, and sometimes we do, but many times we don't have a clue what to say, what to pray, or what to do. Praying in tongues primes the pump of prayer answers at our most desperate point.

The Passion Translation puts it this way: *"The Holy Spirit takes hold of us in our human frailty to empower us in our weakness. For example, at times we don't even know how to pray, or know the best things to ask for. But the Holy Spirit rises up within us to super-intercede on our behalf, pleading to God with emotional sighs too deep for words."*

Super-intercede. I like that! The Holy Spirit is our Super Intercessor and His prayers travel faster than the speed of light. When we can't find human words, the Holy Spirit has plenty of words if we will yield our voice to His utterance.

The Message offers, *"If we don't know how or what to pray, it doesn't matter. He does our praying in and for us, making prayer out of our wordless sighs, our aching groans. He knows us far better than we know ourselves, knows our pregnant condition, and keeps us present before God. That's why we can be so sure that every detail in our lives of love for God is worked into something good."*

The whole creation is groaning, but we can groan in prayer with the Holy Spirit and see His will come to pass in our life even in the most turbulent times. The Holy Spirit is perfect in all of His ways and perfect in all that He prays. He has your best interests in His heart and mind. In times of crisis, praying in tongues is often the most strategic way to pray.

If you are not getting prayer answers, consider what James 4:3 says about "asking amiss." The Greek word for "amiss" in the context of this Scripture means "improperly" or "wrongly," according to the *KJV New Testament Greek Lexicon*. If you are praying wrongly, you won't get the right answers—or perhaps any answer. But if you pray in tongues, you'll get the perfect answer at the perfect time.

Build Up Holy Faith

The Holy Spirit helps us build our faith. Not just any kind of faith—holy faith. In my book *Faith Magnified*, I talk about the concept of hybrid faith. Hybrid faith is a contaminated faith. A hybrid is something that is mixed, like two animals or two vegetables that have characteristics one of another but aren't purely either. Maybe you've heard of pluots. It's a mix of a plumb and an apricot. Seedless watermelons are also a hybrid fruit.

Hybrid foods are devoid of proper mineral balance that all wild foods contain. Hybrid faith is much the same. It's high in doubt and off in faith ratios. Hybrid faith is devoid of proper faith balance—which is 100 percent faith. So when we move in hybrid faith, it leads to a deficiency in the ability to receive what we need from God. Hybrid faith won't move mountains. Seed faith—holy and pure faith—moves mountains.

Jude 20 says, *"But you, beloved, building yourselves up on your most holy faith, praying in the Holy Spirit."* The Amplified Bible, Classic Edition says, *"But you, beloved, build yourselves up [founded] on your most holy faith [make progress, rise like an edifice higher and higher], praying in the Holy Spirit."* And *The Passion Translation* offers, *"But you, my delightfully loved friends, constantly and progressively build yourselves up on the foundation of your most holy faith by praying every moment in the Spirit."*

To build up is to develop gradually by increments; to promote the health, strength, esteem, or reputation of; to accumulate or develop appreciably according to *Merriam-Webster's Dictionary*. Your most holy faith is pure faith. It's not diluted with fear and doubt and unbelief. When you pray in the spirit, you root out the fear, doubt, and unbelief. You are purifying your heart. You are building holy faith. In times of crisis, we need to build our faith to new heights.

Fortify Your Spirit Spiritual Armor

Praying in the spirit fortifies our spiritual armor—and we need strong armor when we're under attack, walking through trials or facing crises. Your armor is complete in Christ, but you can strengthen it by praying in tongues. Consider what God has offered you in Ephesians 6:12-18 (TPT):

> *Your hand-to-hand combat is not with human beings, but with the highest principalities and authorities operating in rebellion under the heavenly realms. For they are a powerful class of demon-gods and evil spirits that hold this dark world in bondage. Because of this, you must wear all the armor that God provides so you're protected as you confront the slanderer, for you are destined for all things and will rise victorious.*

"Put on truth as a belt to strengthen you to stand in triumph. Put on holiness as the protective armor that covers your heart.

Stand on your feet alert, then you'll always be ready to share the blessings of peace. In every battle, take faith as your wrap-around shield, for it is able to extinguish the blazing arrows coming at you from the Evil One! Embrace the power of salvation's full deliverance, like a helmet to *protect your thoughts from lies*. And take the mighty razor-sharp Spirit-sword of the spoken Word of God. Pray passionately in the Spirit, as you constantly intercede with every form of prayer at all times."

Catch that. Pray passionately in the spirit. The New American Standard Bible says *"pray at all times in the Spirit."* The Contemporary English Version offers, "Always pray by the power of the Spirit." Spirit prayer—praying in tongues—is the secret weapon that strengthens the whole armor of God. When we pray in tongues, it helps renew our mind to the truth so our enemy can't remove the God-given belt. When we pray in tongues, we're convinced of our righteousness in Christ (see John 16:8). When we pray in tongues, we enter His rest and peace. When we pray in tongues, it builds up our faith. Can you see it?

Sensitive to the Father's Love

When we pray in tongues, we become more aware of, more sensitive to the Father's love. When we are more sensitive to His love, our faith rises because faith works by love (see Gal. 5:6). When we build our faith, we can build our trust and reject fear. First John 4:18 says, "There is no fear in love; but perfect love casts out fear, because fear involves torment. But he who fears has not been made perfect in love."

In times of crisis perhaps more than ever, we need a revelation of the Father's love. We need to know a love that passes head knowledge and fills our heart with hope. Inspired by the Holy Spirit, Paul—the apostle who said he prayed in tongues more than anyone (see 1 Cor. 14:18)—wrote these pivotal words: "Now hope does not disappoint, because the love of God has been poured out in our hearts by the Holy Spirit who was given to us" (Rom. 5:5).

The New Living Translation says, "And this hope will *not lead to disappointment. For we know how dearly God loves us, because he has given us the Holy Spirit to fill our hearts with h*is love."

The Amplified Bible, Classic Edition puts it this way, *"Such hope never disappoints or deludes or shames us, for God's love has been poured out in our hearts through the Holy Spirit Who has been given to us."*

In times of crisis, we need to be convinced that God loves us. Praying in tongues builds in us a revelation, sensitivity, awareness, and faith of how much God loves us. It helps Romans 8:35-39 get from our head to our heart. These Scriptures read:

> *Who shall separate us from the love of Christ? Shall tribulation, or distress, or persecution, or famine, or nakedness, or peril, or sword? As it is written: 'For Your sake we are killed all day long; We are accounted as sheep for the slaughter.' Yet in all these things we are more than conquerors through Him who loved us. For I am persuaded that neither death nor life, nor angels nor principalities nor powers, nor things present nor*

things to come, nor height nor depth, nor any other created thing, shall be able to separate us from the love of God which is in Christ Jesus our Lord.

Hear God's Voice More Clearly

We all want to hear God's voice more clearly. How much more is this true in times of crisis? Thank God, we have a promise from Jesus that the Holy Spirit will relay His messages. Our spiritual ears are more inclined to His voice when we pray in tongues.

In John 16:13-14 Jesus comforts us with these words: *"However, when He, the Spirit of truth, has come, He will guide you into all truth; for He will not speak on His own authority, but whatever He hears He will speak; and He will tell you things to come. He will glorify*

Me, for He will take of what is Mine and declare it to you."

The more sensitive you are to the Holy Spirit within you, the easier it will be to hear the voice of God speaking to you. The Holy Spirit is God and He speaks to you as a representative of Jesus. The Holy Spirit is your personal prophet!

The New Living Translation of this verse reads: *"When the Spirit of truth comes, he will guide you into all truth. He will not speak on his own but will tell you what he has heard. He will tell you about the future. He will bring me glory by telling you whatever he receives from me."* Praying in tongues helps you tap into that voice of truth.

The Amplified Bible, Classic Edition really amplifies this: *"But when He, the Spirit of Truth (the Truth-giving Spirit) comes, He will guide you into all the Truth (the whole, full Truth). For He will not speak His own message [on His own authority]; but He will tell whatever He hears [from the Father; He will give the message that has been given to Him], and He will announce and declare to you the things that are to come [that will happen in the future]."*

Remember when Jesus said, *"My sheep hear My voice, and I know them, and they follow Me"* (John 10:27)? The Holy Spirit transmits the voice of Jesus to your spirit. Praying in tongues gives you a stronger antenna to pick up that voice clearly. (You can find my webinar, *Hearing God's Voice in Times of Crisis*, at schoolofthespirit.tv.)

Tap Into God's Peace

Praying in tongues helps you tap into the peace of God. You are a citizen of heaven, and peace is your portion. After all, Paul wrote, *"For the kingdom of God is not eating and drinking, but righteousness and peace and joy in the Holy Spirit"* (Rom. 14:17). But in times of crisis the enemy seems to work overtime to steal our peace, kill our tranquility, and destroy serenity.

Think about it. The Holy Spirit is the Spirit of peace. When you pray in the Spirit—when you pray in tongues—you are tapping into the very Spirit of peace. When you feel anxious, you can cast your cares on the Lord and pray in the Spirit and peace will come.

Isaiah 26:3 tells us, *"You will keep him in perfect peace, whose mind is stayed on You, because he trusts in You."* When you have lost your peace, praying in the spirit demonstrates an effort to put your mind on God and trust Him. And Colossians 3:15

suggests, *"And let the peace of God rule in your hearts, to which also you were called in one body; and be thankful."*

When we pray in the spirit, we are choosing peace. We could be speaking words of worry but instead we are speaking words that edify us. We may not understand what we are praying, but we are choosing peace.

Peace can be hard to come by in a chaotic world; how much more so in times of crisis? The enemy sets you up to get you upset and steal your peace. But Jesus left His peace with us and the Spirit of Peace has made His home in us (see John 14:27). We must learn to appropriate the peace of God. We can do that by thanking Him for His peace, but we can also do that by praying in tongues.

When we pray in tongues, we are demonstrating a desire to be spiritually minded. Romans 8:6 makes this promise, *"For to be carnally minded is death, but to be spiritually minded is life and peace."* When you are praying in the spirit, you are being spiritually minded and it leads to peace when stress and worry are trying to overcome you.

Paul tells us in Philippians 4:6-7, *"Be anxious for nothing, but in everything by prayer and supplication, with thanksgiving, let your requests be made known to God; and the peace of God, which surpasses all understanding, will guard your hearts and minds through Christ Jesus."*

Sometimes we cast our cares and take them back, or we try to cast our cares but just can't seem to cast them far enough away from our soul to stop thinking about them. Praying in tongues helps us tap into the peace of God that passes all understanding that guards our hearts and minds through Christ Jesus.

Help Walking Through Tribulation

In John 16:33, Jesus said, *"These things I have spoken to you, that in Me you may have peace. In the world you will have tribulation; but be of good cheer, I have overcome the world."* We all have trials, crises, tribulations, tests, and the like. Praying in tongues can help us walk through trials, crises, tribulations, and tests.

Praying in tongues helps us walk through our trials. It strengthens us to endure the tribulation. Tribulation will come. There is no avoiding it. When the trials hit, we usually have no idea how to pray. Praying in tongues helps us to be of good cheer in the trial.

The Amplified Bible, Classic Edition really draws out these important words of Jesus, *"In the world you have tribulation and trials and distress and frustration; but be of good cheer [take courage; be confident, certain, undaunted]! For I have overcome the world. [I have deprived it of power to harm you and have conquered it for you.]"*

Of course, not every tribulation is earth shattering; some of them are just distress. Some of what we consider tribulation is nothing more than daily frustrations. But those frustrations can mount up. The enemy loves to make a mountain out of a molehill. Praying in tongues in the midst of the crisis helps us to take courage, be confident, certain, and undaunted.

I like that word *undaunted*. It means, "courageously resolute especially in the face of danger or difficulty: not discouraged," according to *Merriam-Webster's Dictionary*. Let's face it, when the crisis comes, sometimes we're daunted. The enemy's fire subdues our fire. But we can choose to pray in tongues and be of good cheer.

The Good News Translation of John 16:33 reads, *"The world will make you suffer. But be brave! I have defeated the world!"* And the New Heart English Bible, *"In the world you have oppression; but cheer up. I have overcome the world."* The Message says, *"In this godless world you will continue to experience difficulties. But take heart! I've conquered the world."* Finally, *The Passion Translation* offers, *"For in this unbelieving world you will experience trouble and sorrows, but you must be courageous, for I have conquered the world!"*

Pray in tongues through your trouble and sorrows! You'll make your way through with more courage. The key is remembering to do that, right? Sometimes in the midst of crisis we forget to do what we know to do. That's why making a habit of praying in tongues is so vital to your successful Christian living. When something is a habit, you don't have to think about it! It just kicks in!

Healing to Your Physical Body

Can you really receive physical healing through praying in tongues? Yes. Absolutely. Emphatically so. Praying in tongues can also set you up to walk in divine health. The Spirit gives life (see John 6:63).

Your body is the temple of the Holy Spirit, according to 1 Corinthians 16:9. The Holy Spirit is interested in living in a healthy house rather than a broken-down house. Praying in tongues can bring healing to your physical body.

Let's dive deeper into this. Jude 20 tell us, *"But you, beloved, building yourselves up on your most holy faith, praying in the Holy Spirit."* The Greek word for "building" in that verse is *epoikodomeo*, which means to build up, according to *The NASB New Testament Greek Lexicon*.

And 1 Corinthians 14:4 tells us, *"He who speaks in a tongue edifies himself."* That Greek word for "edifies" in that verse is *oikodomeo*. According to The *KJV New Testament Greek Lexicon*, edify in this verse means, "to build a house, erect a building" and "to restore by building, to rebuild, repair." So when you pray in tongues, the Holy Spirit is not just building you up, He's rebuilding and repairing His temple.

We know it's God's will to heal. First Peter 2:24 clearly says, Jesus *"Himself bore our sins in His own body on the tree, that we, having died to sins, might live for righteousness—by whose stripes you were healed."* If you were healed when Jesus took those 39 lashes on His body then died on a cross to pay the price for your sin—and you were—then you are healed now. You have to, though, extend faith for healing.

When we pray in tongues, we are not just building ourselves up in our most holy faith, we are rebuilding our health. When you pray in tongues with a mind toward healing, I believe the Holy Spirit also joins with your prayer. And Psalm 103:2-4 reads, *"Bless the Lord, O my soul, and forget not all His benefits: who forgives all your iniquities, who heals all your diseases, who redeems your life from destruction."* When you pray in tongues, you are tapping into these benefits and into healing power when your body needs it.

Intercede for Others

We're all called to make intercession. Intercession is merely praying for others. It's pleading someone's case to God. In 1 Timothy 2:1, Paul tells us, *"Therefore I exhort first of all that supplications, prayers, intercessions, and giving of thanks be made for all men."* And Ephesians 6:18 tells us we should be, *"Praying always with all prayer and supplication in the Spirit, being watchful to this end with all perseverance and supplication for all the saints."*

In times of crisis, you can be like Jesus and serve as an intercessor. When we make intercession, we're acting like Christ. Jesus isn't just sitting at the right hand of the Father waiting for His opportunity to come back and face the devil for a third time. No, Hebrews 7:25 tells us He always lives to make intercession for us.

Romans 8:34 tells us, *"Who is he who condemns? It is Christ who died, and furthermore is also risen, who is even at the right hand of God, who also makes intercession for us."* When we are standing in the role of intercessor, we are exercising a ministry that our Lord Jesus Christ is also actively demonstrating in heaven.

Indeed, intercession is a selfless act. Here's the thing: Christ knows exactly how to intercede for anyone or anything. He always releases a perfect prayer. But we don't always know how to make intercession for something or someone. We don't always know how to pray. Sometimes we can see a need and pray accurately, but sometimes there are unseen needs or we just flat out don't know how to respond rightly in prayer. Thank God for the promise in Romans 8:26:

> *Likewise, the Spirit helps us in our weaknesses, for we do not know what to pray for as we ought, but the Spirit Himself intercedes for us with groanings too deep for words* (MEV).

When we pray in the spirit, we're praying a perfect prayer according to God's will, and that works just as well when we are praying for ourselves as when we are praying for others.

The Contemporary English Version of this verse reads: *"In certain ways we are weak, but the Spirit is here to help us. For example, when we don't know what to pray for, the Spirit prays for us in ways that cannot be put into words."* How do you intercede for someone by praying in tongues? We can lift up someone's name and tell God we don't know how to pray for them with our natural understanding, then ask the Holy Spirit to help us pray for them as we give utterance to tongues.

The Good News Translation puts it this way: *"In the same way the Spirit also comes to help us, weak as we are. For we do not know how we ought to pray; the Spirit himself pleads with God for us in groans that words cannot express."*

The Holy Spirit can plead for them through us. We may never know what we prayed. We might not be daring enough to pray in English what we prayed in the Spirit. We might not even think it's the best way to pray if we did know what we were praying. So our mind is unfruitful, but the prayer is perfect.

In *Transform: A 90-Day Spirit Prayer Challenge*, I offer 90 teachings on what praying in tongues does. These truths have transformed the lives of believers around the world. You can find this challenge at www.schoolofthespirit.tv.

Chapter 4

Getting Filled with the Spirit

Before Jesus hung on a cross, He comforted His disciples with an epic promise. We find that promise in John 14:16-17, *"And I will pray the Father, and He will give you another Helper, that He may abide with you forever—the Spirit of truth, whom the world cannot receive, because it neither sees Him nor knows Him; but you know Him, for He dwells with you and will be in you."*

The Holy Spirit is that Helper; He is the Spirit of truth. The Holy Spirit dwells with every believer, but there is a difference between water baptism and the baptism of the Holy Spirit. John the Baptist told His disciples that Jesus would come to baptize believers in the Holy Spirit (see Mark 1:8). The first baptism was on Pentecost Sunday in the Upper Room. We read the account in Acts 2:1-4:

> *When the Day of Pentecost had fully come, they were all with one accord in one place. And suddenly there came a sound from heaven, as of a rushing mighty wind, and it filled the whole house where they were sitting. Then there appeared to them divided tongues, as of fire, and one sat upon each of them. And they were all filled with the Holy Spirit and began to speak with other tongues, as the Spirit gave them utterance.*

You can't pray in tongues unless you are baptized in the Holy Spirit. But when you are baptized in Him, Jesus promised, *"He who believes in Me, as the Scripture has said, out of his heart will flow rivers of living water.' But this He spoke concerning the Spirit, whom those believing in Him would receive; for the Holy Spirit was not yet given, because Jesus was not yet glorified"* (John 7:37-39).

How to Get Filled with the Spirit

You may have to renew your mind about lies you have heard about speaking in tongues. My grandfather told me it was of the devil, and when I saw people pray in tongues it frightened me. That's what the enemy wants. I had to renew my mind with Scriptures before I could ever receive this heavenly baptism.

First, you need to believe that God gave the gift of the Holy Spirit at Pentecost—and this wasn't a one-time outpouring of the Holy Spirit. This gift has been available to all believers in Jesus Christ since that day.

You receive the Holy Spirit by faith, just like you received your salvation. We don't have to beg God to give us the Holy Spirit. We don't have to tarry for days and years. Faith doesn't beg. Faith believes and receives.

Consider Jesus' words in Luke 11:11-13, *"If a son asks for bread from any father among you, will he give him a stone? Or if he asks for a fish, will he give him a serpent instead of a fish? Or if he asks for an egg, will he offer him a scorpion? If you then, being evil, know how to give good gifts to your children, how much more will your heavenly Father give the Holy Spirit to those who ask Him!"*

Second, you don't have to be living perfect to receive the Holy Spirit any more than you need to be living perfect to get saved. The Holy Spirit Himself perfects you. He sanctifies you little by little. He is your Helper and wants to help you. He can help you more if you are filled with Him.

Put another way, we don't work for the Holy Spirit—we receive Him as a gift from the Father, as another Comforter that Christ talked about.

Third, you can receive the Holy Spirit through the laying on of hands, but that's not the only way to be baptized. Back in the Voice of Healing days, Oral Roberts and other televangelists would tell people to put their hands on the TV screen as a point of contact and they would be filled to overflowing. I was baptized in the Holy Spirit at a Joyce Meyer conference. No one laid hands on me at all.

We see this type of baptism in the Holy Spirit in Acts 10:44-46: *"While Peter was still speaking these words, the Holy Spirit fell upon all those who heard the word. And those of the circumcision who believed were astonished, as many as came with Peter, because the gift of the Holy Spirit had been poured out on the Gentiles also. For they heard them speak with tongues and magnify God."*

Fourth, after you ask to be filled with the Spirit, you will have to do something. You will have to take a step of faith. You may feel a bubbling up in your spirit. You may feel tingly or warm. Or you may not feel anything. You'll have to open your mouth and yield it to the Holy Spirit. You do the talking as the Holy Spirit gives you utterance.

Getting Filled with the Spirit

Psalm 81:10 tells us, *"Open your mouth wide, and I will fill it."* Open your mouth and release your voice to the Holy Spirit. It may sound at first like baby talk or gibberish. That's OK. Just like a baby's language grows and develops, so will your prayer language over time. Remember, we are speaking. The Holy Spirit is not speaking. We are speaking and He is giving us utterance. An utterance is a vocal expression, power, style, or manner of speaking, according to *Merriam-Webster's Dictionary*.

Prayer for a Fresh Infilling

Jesus is the Baptizer, and He baptizes us with the Holy Spirit when we ask and believe. Even if you've been filled with the Spirit, you may need to get refilled. As it has been said, we're all a little leaky. We fill up our cars with gas, and we need to fill up our spirit with the Holy Spirit who quickens our mortal bodies.

Ephesians 5:18-19 confirms this: "And do not be drunk with wine, in which is dissipation; but be filled with the Spirit, speaking to one another in psalms and hymns and spiritual songs, singing and making melody in your heart to the Lord." When Paul wrote be filled, the tense expresses the reality of being continually filled. It's not a one-time event. In the Book of Acts, we see the apostles were filled multiple times.

If you have not been filled with the Spirit and you want to be, pray this prayer:

Father, I surrender full control of my life to You. I ask You even now to fill me to overflowing with Your Spirit, just as You have promised to do if I ask according to Your will. I ask this in the name of Jesus and believe that You are pouring out your Spirit upon me right now.

Now, take a deep breath as if you are breathing in the Holy Spirit. I often tell people to drink deep. Jesus told people to come and drink, and He was speaking of drinking of the river of life, which you breathe in. Open your mouth and He will fill it. If nothing seems to be happening, relax and don't get in your mind about it. Don't get in unbelief about it. Sometimes you'll hear the words on the inside and you have to give voice to them. Speak out in faith.

Your Heavenly Prayer Language

Paul shared a marvelous revelation in 1 Corinthians 14:2, *"For he who speaks in an unknown tongue does not speak to men, but to God. For no one understands him, although in the spirit, he speaks mysteries*" (MEV). That word *unknown* is in italics in many Bible translations because it doesn't appear in the original text. Translators added it in. It's not an unknown tongue. It's a heavenly language.

It is unknown in the sense that it's not known to the people around you. It's known between you and God. Your tongues for personal edification sound different than other people's tongues for personal edification because it's your personal gift from God expressing Himself through you to Him.

I pray in the Spirit as much as I possibly can. I wake up most mornings and pray at least 30 minutes in the Spirit before doing anything else. You can too. I pray in the Spirit while I am in my car driving from place to place. You can too. I even broke out in tongues on the treadmill at the gym accidentally—because it's automatic. It can be for you too. You can choose to give voice to the Holy Spirit's utterance. You can choose to pray in tongues.

Chapter 5
Prophecies to War With

We've focused on praying in tongues, but you can also pray in the Spirit in English. Many times when I pray in tongues, I launch out into Spirit-led prayer in my own language. Another strategic way to pray in the Spirit in times of crisis is to pray through prophetic words.

You can also war with prophetic words. Paul taught his spiritual son Timothy this principle in 1 Timothy 1:18 (AMPC), *"This charge and admonition I commit in trust to you, Timothy, my son, in accordance with prophetic intimations which I formerly received concerning you, so that inspired and aided by them you may wage the good warfare."*

I've chosen a few entries from my *Victory Decrees: Daily Prophetic Strategies for Spiritual Warfare Victory* devotional. I read from this every morning on my devotional prayer call. These entries are prophetic words the Holy Spirit spoke to my heart, along with prayers you can pray and decrees you can make over your life in times of crisis.

Wear the Cloak of Zeal

Christ wore a cloak of zeal. He is a zealous warrior who never loses a battle. You can choose when you are weary to put on that same cloak. You can operate in fervent faith. You can choose to rise up with a passion and urgency to dismantle the devil's work against your life. But you have to put on the cloak. You have to stir yourself up. You have to build yourself up in your most holy faith, praying in the spirit and encouraging yourself in My Word like David did. Put on the cloak of zeal and take down every Goliath in your life. I am your victory banner.

> *Father, in the name of Jesus, adorn me with Your cloak of zeal and give me a sense of urgency about the enemy's work against me. Help me stay alert and stirred up in my spirit. I decree the enemy's fervor against me is no match for the favor of God that rests upon me. I declare zeal for God's house consumes me, in Jesus' name.*

Don't You Think I Have a Plan?

Don't you think I have a plan? Yes, indeed, I do have a plan for you that exceeds anything you could ever ask for or imagine. Don't give up just shy of the breakthrough. Don't stop praying. Don't stop pushing. If you could just see what I see instead of what the enemy is showing you, you would put your mouth in line with My Word. If you could just look beyond the enemy's smoke and mirrors, you would rejoice. You would dance. You would shout. You would leap. You would call and tell all your friends of My goodness. So look by faith and rejoice because the enemy cannot stop My plans for you unless you let him. Don't let him.

Father, would You give me a glimpse of plans You have hidden from the enemy? Would You let me peek at what's next so I can prepare for the battle against it? I decree the warfare against God's plan for my life ricochets back to the enemy. I declare God's plans are higher than my plans—and they are good, in Jesus' name.

Ask for My Will

Asking for My will in your fight is an assault on the enemy's kingdom because it unlocks My will for your life in the earth. Ask and receive that your joy may be made full. Pray bold prayers. Pray accurate prayers. Pray with the end in mind. See My will in your heart and pray My will through your mouth, then do it again and again and again. Ask and keep on asking. You can ask Me anything. I am listening to your heart's cries. I am working all things together for good. Keep making the ask. Let's start praying.

Father, help me pray with the end in mind. Help me see Your will for my life and give me the tenacity to ask and keep on asking even when I don't see things changing. I decree the enemy of God's will for my life is ashamed and confused by his own audacity. I declare God hears me and answers me when I call, in Jesus' name.

Jesus Is Praying for You

The enemy will come from time to time to sift you like wheat. The enemy sifted Job and he saw things in himself he didn't like. The enemy sifted Peter and he saw things in himself that he never knew were there. The enemy will come at times to sift you, but remember—Jesus is praying for you. The enemy will come to test you and try you, working to find a place in you, hoping to cause you to deny Christ, to depart the faith, to give up on the hope of glory. Hold on to Me. I am holding on to you. The sifting will purify you and give you strength.

Father, strengthen me through the times of sifting so I can withstand the attack of the enemy against my faith. Purify my heart and I will worship You all the more. I decree my faith shall not be shipwrecked but it grows stronger as I meditate on God's Word. I declare the sifting will lead to a shifting toward greater victory, in Jesus' name.

I Am Dispatching Angels

I'm sending angelic assistance your way. I'm dispatching to you angels on assignment just for you. I'm releasing the angels of breakthrough into your life. Don't stop praying now. The angels are coming on assignment because of your words. Don't shrink back from the battle. Help from the heavenly host is on the way. Don't pull back and don't cease fire. You are on the brink of victory. Don't let your foot off the gas. You are speeding forth into triumph. Keep pressing. Keep praying. Angels are encamped around you even now because you fear Me.

> *Father, release Your heavenly host to help me fight against the demon powers that have eyes set on my destruction. Dispatch the warring angels on my behalf. I decree God's angels on assignment overpower every attack against me. I declare angels hearken to the voice of God's Word in my mouth, in Jesus' name.*

**YOU CAN PICK UP YOUR COPY OF
VICTORY DECREES FOR MORE ENTRIES LIKE THIS.**

About the Author

Jennifer is senior leader of Awakening House of Prayer in Fort Lauderdale, FL, founder of the Ignite Network, and founder of the Awakening Blaze prayer movement. Jennifer formerly served as the first-ever female editor of *Charisma* magazine and is a prolific author of over 25 books. You can find Jennifer online or shoot her an email at info@jenniferleclaire.org.

Made in the USA
Columbia, SC
31 May 2020